Zaner-Bloser
Handwriting
With a new alphabet

Author

Clinton S. Hackney

Contributing Authors

Pamela J. Farris
Janice T. Jones
Linda Leonard Lamme

Zaner-Bloser, Inc., P.O. Box 16764, Columbus, Ohio 43216-6764   1-800-421-3018

Copyright © 1996 Zaner-Bloser, Inc.   ISBN 0-88085-730-7

Developed by Kirchoff/Wohlberg, Inc., in cooperation with Zaner-Bloser Publishers

Printed in the United States of America

97 98 99 WC 5 4 3 2

You already know handwriting is important.
Now take a look at...

NEW
Zaner-Bloser Handwriting

Easier to read!   Easier to write!   Easier to teach!

I see Zaner-Bloser's alphabet in the books I read.

I like Zaner-Bloser because it's so easy to write.

Zaner-Bloser's new program is easy to teach.

ii

You already know handwriting is important, but did you know...

Did You Know...

Annually, the U.S. Postal Service receives 38 million illegibly addressed letters, costing American taxpayers $4 million each year.

–*American Demographics*, Dec. 1992

Did You Know...

Hundreds of thousands of tax returns are delayed every year because figures, notes, and signatures are illegible.

–*Better Handwriting in 30 Days*, 1989

Did You Know...

Poor handwriting costs American business $200 million annually.

–*American Demographics*, Dec. 1992

Zaner-Bloser's CONTINUOUS-STROKE manuscript alphabet

Aa Bb Cc Dd Ee Ff Gg
Oo Pp Qq Rr Ss Tt

Easier to Read

Our vertical manuscript alphabet is like the alphabet kids see every day inside and outside of the classroom. They see it in their school books, in important environmental print like road signs, and in books and cartoons they read for fun.

"[Slanted] manuscript is not only harder to learn than traditional [vertical] print, but it creates substantially more letter recognition errors and causes more letter confusion than does the traditional style."

–Debby Kuhl and Peter Dewitz in a paper presented at the 1994 meeting of the American Educational Research Association

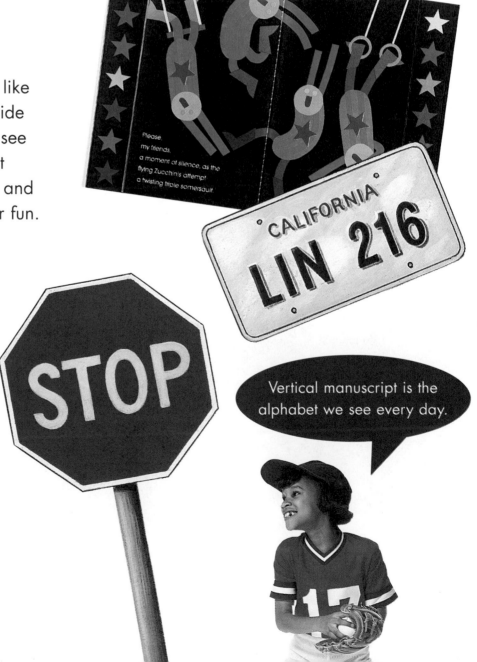

Please, my friends, a moment of silence, as the flying Zucchinis attempt a twisting triple somersault.

CALIFORNIA LIN 216

STOP

Vertical manuscript is the alphabet we see every day.

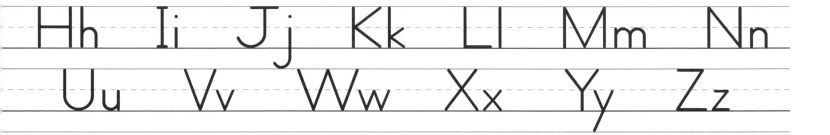

Hh Ii Jj Kk Ll Mm Nn
Uu Vv Ww Xx Yy Zz

Easier to Write

Our vertical manuscript alphabet is written with continuous strokes—fewer pencil lifts—so there's a greater sense of flow in writing. And kids can write every letter once they learn four simple strokes that even kindergartners can manage.

Four simple strokes: circle, horizontal line, vertical line, slanted line

"The writing hand has to change direction more often when writing the [slanted] alphabet, do more retracing of lines, and make more strokes that occur later in children's development."

–Steve Graham in *Focus on Exceptional Children*, 1992

Many kids can already write their names when they start school (vertical manuscript).

Kirk

Why should they have to relearn them in another form (slanted manuscript)? With Zaner-Bloser, they don't have to.

Kirk

Easier to Teach

Our vertical manuscript alphabet is easy to teach because there's no reteaching involved. Children are already familiar with our letterforms—they've seen them in their environment and they've learned them at home.

"Before starting school, many children learn how to write traditional [vertical] manuscript letters from their parents or preschool teachers. Learning a special alphabet such as [slanted] means that these children will have to relearn many of the letters they can already write."

–Steve Graham in *Focus on Exceptional Children*, 1992

Zaner-Bloser's NEW SIMPLIFIED cursive alphabet

$\mathcal{A}a$ $\mathcal{B}b$ $\mathcal{C}c$ $\mathcal{D}d$ $\mathcal{E}e$ $\mathcal{F}f$ $\mathcal{G}g$

$\mathcal{N}n$ $\mathcal{O}o$ $\mathcal{P}p$ $\mathcal{Q}q$ $\mathcal{R}r$ $\mathcal{S}s$

Simplified letterforms...
Easier to read and write

old letterform

Letterforms are simplified so they're easier to write and easier to identify in writing. The new simplified **Q** now looks like a **Q** instead of a number 2.

old letterform

Our simplified letterforms use the headline, midline, and baseline as a guide for where letters start and stop. The new simplified **d** touches the headline instead of stopping halfway.

old letterform

No more "cane stems!" Our new simplified letterforms begin with a small curve instead of fancy loops that can be difficult for students to write.

vi

Hh Ii Jj Kk Ll Mm
Tt Uu Vv Ww Xx Yy Zz

Simplified letterforms...
Easier to teach

When handwriting is easy for students to write, instruction time is cut way back! That's the teaching advantage with Zaner-Bloser Handwriting. Our cursive letterforms are simplified so instead of spending a lot of time teaching fancy loops that give kids trouble, teachers give instruction for simple, basic handwriting that students can use for the rest of their lives.

And remember, with Zaner-Bloser Handwriting, students learn to write manuscript with continuous strokes. That means that when it's time for those students to begin writing cursive, the transition comes naturally because they already know the flow of continuous strokes.

These simple letters are so much easier to teach!

The Student Edition...set up for student success

Letters are grouped and taught by the strokes used to form them.

Letter models show stroke direction and sequence.

Students first practice letters, then joinings, and finally complete words and sentences.

Write Doublecurve and Overcurve Letters

T, F, I, and Q are not joined to the letter that follows.
J is joined to the letter that follows.

Write the letters, joinings, and words. Then write the sentences.

T   T   T   T   Tibet   Tonga

F   F   F   F   Fiji   Falkland Islands

I   I   I   I   Italy   India

Q   Q   Q   Quebec   Quito

J   J   J   Ju   Ja   Jo

San Juan   Japan   Jordan

DID YOU KNOW?

Tonga is part of Polynesia.

Fiji is part of Melanesia.

EVALUATE Circle your best word.

20

Grade 6 Student Edition

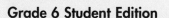

Write an Outline

An outline is a writing plan. Here is the first part of an outline for a report on family names.

What's in a Name? ← title
I. History of Family Names ← main topic
  A. Beginnings ← subtopic
    1 Chinese—first to have more than one name ← detail
    2 Roman Empire—used three names
  B. Middle Ages

Use the details listed below to complete the second part of the outline. As you write, pay attention to the size and shape of your letters.

Yamashita—below the mountain   Barker—shepherd
Chandler—candlemaker   Bach—lives by the brook

II. Sources of Family Names
  A. Father's name
    1 Karlsdotter—daughter of Karl
    2 Ben-David—son of David
  B. Occupational names
    1
    2
  C. Place names
    1
    2

EVALUATE Are your short letters half the height of your tall letters?   Yes   No

30

Language arts connections are easy with activities like this one. Here students learn how to write an outline as they practice their handwriting.

Grade 6 Student Edition

Write Complex Sentences

Two sentences can be combined to form a complex sentence.

Do as the Romans do when you're in Rome.

Use the word in parentheses to combine each pair of sentences.

It is not considered rude to stare at other people. You are in Pakistan. (if)

_____

_____

Polite Japanese women cover their mouths. They laugh. (when)

_____

_____

A horizontal shake of the head means "no." You are in Sri Lanka or Bulgaria. (unless)

_____

_____

On Your Own Write a complex sentence. Use the connecting word *because*.

_____

_____

EVALUATE Is there space for ○ between letters?   Yes   No
Is there space for ＼ between words?   Yes   No

39

Grade 6 Student Edition

Write in Spanish

What is today's date?
¿Qué día es hoy?

		Sunday January 19___	Wednesday February 19___
		1	**28**

Monday	lunes
Tuesday	martes
Wednesday	miércoles
Thursday	jueves
Friday	viernes
Saturday	sábado
Sunday	domingo
January	enero
February	febrero
March	marzo
April	abril
May	mayo
June	junio
July	julio
August	agosto
September	septiembre
October	octubre
November	noviembre
December	diciembre

domingo
1 de enero

miércoles
28 de febrero

Write each date in Spanish. Use the word keys to help you.

Monday, September 5

Thursday, November 23

Sunday, January 15

Tuesday, May 30

Wednesday, June 14

Saturday, April 1

On Your Own ¿Qué día es hoy? Answer in Spanish.

_____

EVALUATE Did you use lowercase cursive letters?   Yes   No
Did you remember to include the accent marks?   Yes   No

34

Grade 6 Student Edition

ix

The Teacher Edition...streamlined instruction

At-a-glance stroke descriptions are short and easy to find.

Visual references to practice masters for each lesson save you time.

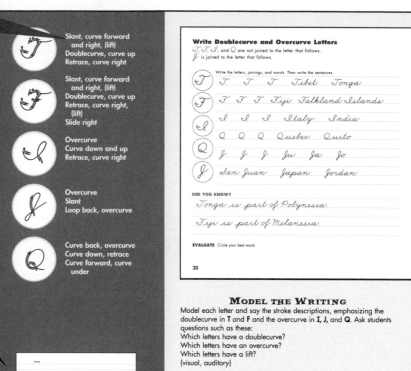

Grade 6 Teacher Edition

Brief teaching notes save you valuable time.

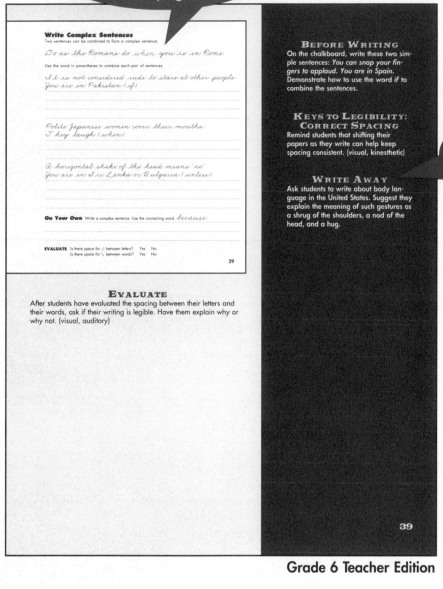

> The student page is close to the instruction for that page.

Write Complex Sentences

Two sentences can be combined to form a complex sentence.

Do as the Romans do when you're in Rome.

Use the word in parentheses to combine each pair of sentences.

It is not considered rude to stare at other people.
You are in Pakistan. (if)

Polite Japanese women cover their mouths.
They laugh. (when)

A horizontal shake of the head means 'no.'
You are in Sri Lanka or Bulgaria. (unless)

On Your Own Write a complex sentence. Use the connecting word *because.*

EVALUATE Is there space for ○ between letters?   Yes   No
Is there space for \ between words?   Yes   No

39

BEFORE WRITING
On the chalkboard, write these two simple sentences: *You can snap your fingers to applaud. You are in Spain.* Demonstrate how to use the word *if* to combine the sentences.

KEYS TO LEGIBILITY:
CORRECT SPACING
Remind students that shifting their papers as they write can help keep spacing consistent. (visual, kinesthetic)

> Language arts connections reinforce writing and other skills.

WRITE AWAY
Ask students to write about body language in the United States. Suggest they explain the meaning of such gestures as a shrug of the shoulders, a nod of the head, and a hug.

EVALUATE
After students have evaluated the spacing between their letters and their words, ask if their writing is legible. Have them explain why or why not. (visual, auditory)

39

Grade 6 Teacher Edition

Grade 6 Practice Masters

An accompanying book of practice masters offers additional practice for every letter and skill students learn. It also includes resources to make teaching easier—certificates, an evaluation record, letters to send home to keep parents and guardians involved, and Spanish activities.

Evaluation and Assessment... consistent guidance throughout the year

Student self-evaluation...

In every lesson. Students evaluate their own handwriting and circle their best work.

In every review. Several times a year, students review the letterforms and joinings they've learned and again evaluate their handwriting.

Through application activities. Students apply what they've learned in relevant practice activities that fill half the book. In each activity, they evaluate their own handwriting.

Teacher assessment...

In every lesson and review. As students evaluate their own writing, teachers can assess their letterforms, as well as their comprehension of good handwriting. Corrective Strategies for each lesson offer teachers helpful hints for common handwriting problems.

Through application activities. Students' work in relevant practice activities offers lots of opportunity for informal assessment of handwriting, language arts, and other areas.

The Keys to Legibility

These four Keys to Legibility are taught and reviewed throughout the program.
They remind students that their goal should be legible handwriting.

Size

Consistently sized letters are easy to read. Students learn to write letterforms that are consistent in size.

Slant

Letters with a consistent slant are easy to read. Students learn how to position their papers and hold their pencils so consistent slant comes with ease.

Shape

Four simple strokes—undercurve, downcurve, overcurve, and slant—make it easy for students to write letters with consistent and proper shape.

Spacing

Correct spacing between letters and words makes handwriting easy to read. Practical hints show students how to determine correct spacing.

Handwriting practice...relevant application

Write a Paragraph

The following sentences tell about different customs for naming children. Put the sentences in a paragraph by adding a topic sentence. Write the complete paragraph.

Many African children receive one name at birth and a second name later on. In China, names for boys are often plain, while names for girls are elaborate. Greek parents traditionally name the firstborn child after a paternal grandparent.

COLLISION ALERT Make sure your tall letters do not bump into the descenders above them.

Different countries have different customs for naming children. Many African children receive one name at birth and a second name later on. In China, names for bo— while names for gi— Greek parents trad— firstborn child after— grandparent.

EVALUATE Did you avoid collisions? (Yes) No
Is your writing legible? (Yes) No

Completed Grade 6 Student Edition

> Students practice their handwriting in relevant ways. Here, they learn how to write a paragraph.

Edit Your Writing

Use these proofreading marks to edit your writing.

≡ Capitalize.   ∧ Insert (add).
/ Use lowercase.   ⋊ Delete (take out).
⊙ Add period.   ¶ Indent for paragraph.

Write this paragraph. Make the changes indicated by the proofreading marks.

¶ Limerick is the ^third^ largest city of the Republic of Ireland. It is also a kinds ^A limerick^ ^form^ of silly poetry which came first. The city or the verse? The verse ^probably^ gets its name from an ^old^ Irish song, "Will You Come Up ⊥o Limerick?"

Limerick is the third largest city of the Republic of Ireland. A limerick is also a form of humorous verse. Which came first, the city or the verse? The verse probably gets its name from an old Irish song, "Will You Come Up to Limerick?"

EVALUATE Ask a friend to proofread your writing.
Is the paragraph written correctly? (Yes) No

32

> In this practice activity, students learn how to edit and rewrite a paragraph.

A huge collection of supplementary materials... makes handwriting even easier to teach!

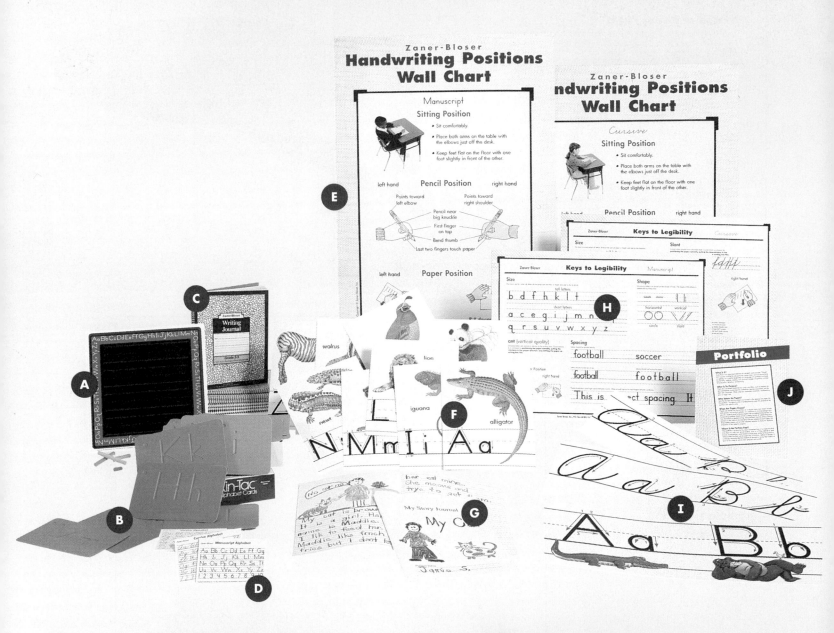

A **Practice Chalkboards** *grades K–4*

B **Manuscript Kin-Tac Cards** *grades K–2*

C **Writing Journals** *grades 1–6*

D **Alphabet Card Set** *grades 1–6*

E **Handwriting Positions Wall Chart** *grades 1–6*

F **Letter Cards** *grades K–2*

G **Story Journals** *grades K–4*

H **Keys to Legibility Wall Chart** *grades 2–6*

I **Alphabet Wall Strips** *grades 1–6*

J **Portfolio Assessment Guide** *grades 1–6*

For more information about these materials, call 1-800-421-3018.

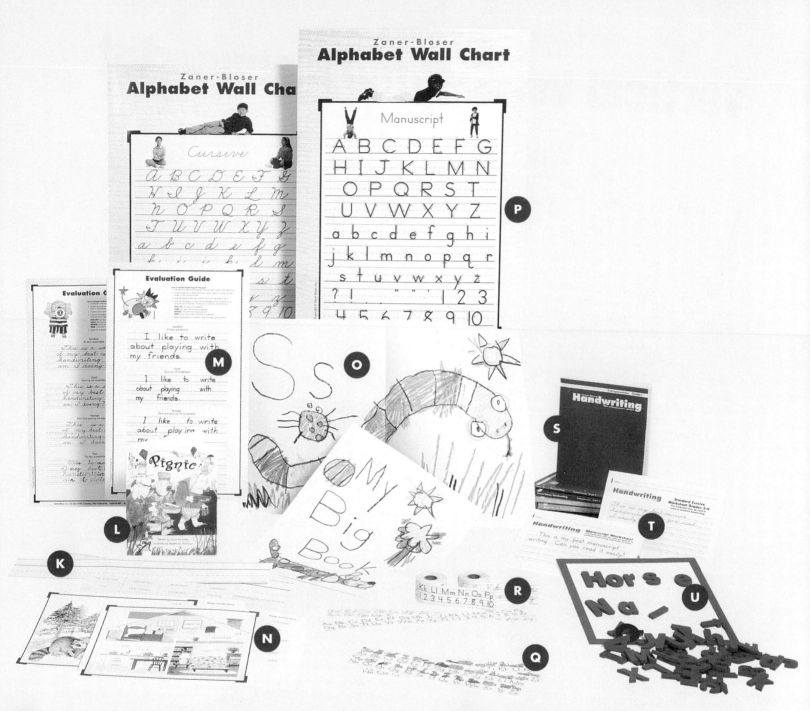

K	**Blank Sentence Strips** *grades K–6*	**Q**	**Illustrated Alphabet Strips** *grades K–2*
L	**Pignic Alphabet Book** *grades K–2*	**R**	**Desk Strips** *grades 1–6*
M	**Evaluation Guides** *grades 1–6*	**S**	**Book of Transparencies** *grades 1–6*
N	**Vinyl Storyboard Set** *grades K–2*	**T**	**Parent/Student Worksheets** *grades 2–6*
O	**Make-Your-Own Big Book** *grades K–2*	**U**	**Write-On, Wipe-Off Magnetic Board With Letters** *grades K–2*
P	**Alphabet Wall Chart** *grades K–4*		

Vertical vs. *Slanted Manuscript*

What the research shows

Using a slanted alphabet has been a trend in handwriting instruction. It's actually not a new development—the first slanted alphabet was created in 1968. A sort of bridge between manuscript and cursive, this slanted alphabet used unconnected letter-forms like the traditional vertical manuscript, but its letterforms were slanted like cursive.

It seemed like a good idea. This alphabet was to be easier to write than cursive, yet similar enough to cursive that children wouldn't learn two *completely* different alphabets. But after several years of use in some schools, research has uncovered some unfortunate findings.

Slanted manuscript can be difficult to write

Slanted manuscript was created to be similar to cursive, so it uses more complicated strokes such as small curves, and these strokes can be difficult for young children.

Vertical manuscript, on the other hand, is consistent with the development of young children. Each of its letters is formed with simple strokes—straight lines, circles, and slanted lines. One researcher found that the strokes used in vertical manuscript are the same as the shapes children use in their drawings (Farris, 1993). Because children are familiar with these shapes, they can identify and form the strokes with little difficulty.

Slanted manuscript can create problems with legibility

Legibility is an important goal in handwriting. Obviously, content should not be sacrificed for legibility, but what is handwriting if it cannot be read?

Educational researchers have tested the legibility of slanted manuscript and found that children writing vertical manuscript "performed significantly better" than those writing slanted manuscript. The writers of the slanted alphabet tended to make more misshapen letterforms, tended to extend their strokes above and below the guidelines, and had a difficult time keeping their letterforms consistent in size (Graham, 1992).

On the other hand, the vertical manuscript style of print has a lot of support in the area of research. Advertisers have known for years that italic type has a lower readability rate than vertical "roman" type. Research shows that in 30 minute readings, the italic style is read 4.9% slower than roman type (14–16 words per minute). This is why most literature, especially literature for early readers, is published using roman type.

Slanted manuscript can impair letter recognition

Educators have suspected that it would be beneficial for students to write and read the same style of alphabet. In other words, if children *read* vertical manuscript, they should also *write* vertical manuscript. Now it has been found that inconsistent alphabets may actually be detrimental to children's learning.

Researchers have found that slanted manuscript impairs the ability of some young children to recognize many letters. Some children who learn the slanted style alphabet find it difficult to recognize many of the traditional letterforms they see in books and environmental print. "[These children] consistently had difficulty identifying several letters, often making the same erroneous response to the same letter," the researchers reported. They concluded that slanted manuscript "creates substantially more letter recognition errors and causes more letter confusion than does the traditional style." (Kuhl & Dewitz, 1994).

Slanted manuscript does not help with transition

One of the benefits proposed by the creators of the slanted manuscript alphabet was that it made it easier for children to make the transition from manuscript to cursive writing. However, no difference in transition time has been found between the two styles of manuscript alphabets. In addition, the slanted style does not seem to enhance young children's production of cursive letters (Graham, 1992).

> *"…slanted manuscript letters cannot be recommended as a replacement for the traditional manuscript alphabet."*

The slanted style of manuscript appeared to be a good idea. But educators should take a close look at what the research shows before adopting this style of alphabet. As one researcher has said, "Given the lack of supportive evidence and the practical problems involved in implementation, slanted manuscript letters cannot be recommended as a replacement for the traditional manuscript alphabet" (Graham, 1994).

Farris, P.J. (1993). Learning to write the ABC's: A comparison of D'Nealian and Zaner-Bloser handwriting styles. *Indiana Reading Quarterly,* 25 (4), 26–33.

Graham, S. (1992). Issues in handwriting instruction. *Focus on Exceptional Children,* 25 (2).

Graham, S. (1994, Winter). Are slanted manuscript alphabets superior to the traditional manuscript alphabet? *Childhood Education,* 91–95.

Kuhl, D. & Dewitz, P. (1994, April). The effect of handwriting style on alphabet recognition. Paper presented at the annual meeting of the American Educational Research Association, New Orleans, LA.

Zaner-Bloser
Handwriting
With a new alphabet

Author
Clinton S. Hackney

Contributing Authors
Pamela J. Farris
Janice T. Jones
Linda Leonard Lamme

Zaner-Bloser, Inc.
P.O. Box 16764
Columbus, Ohio 43216-6764

Author

Clinton S. Hackney, Ed.D.

Contributing Authors

Pamela J. Farris, Ph.D.
Janice T. Jones, M.A.
Linda Leonard Lamme, Ph.D.

Reviewers

Judy L. Bausch, Grade 6, Columbus, Georgia
Cherlynn Bruce, Grade I, Conroe, Texas
Karen H. Burke, Director of Curriculum and Instruction,
Bar Mills, Maine
Anne Chamberlin, Grade 2, Lynchburg, Virginia
Carol J. Fuhler, Grade 6, Flagstaff, Arizona
Deborah D. Gallagher, Grade 5, Gainesville, Florida
Kathleen Harrington, Grade 3, Redford, Michigan
Rebecca James, Grade 3, East Greenbush, New York
Gerald R. Maeckelbergh, Principal, Blaine, Minnesota
Bessie B. Peabody, Principal, East St. Louis, Illinois

Marilyn S. Petruska, Grade 5, Coraopolis, Pennsylvania
Sharon Ralph, Kindergarten, Nashville, Tennessee
Linda E. Ritchie, Grade 4, Birmingham, Alabama
Roberta Hogan Royer, Grade 2, North Canton, Ohio
Marion Redmond Starks, Grade 2, Baltimore, Maryland
Elizabeth J. Taglieri, Grade 2, Lake Zurich, Illinois
Claudia Williams, Grade 6, Lewisburg, West Virginia

Credits

Art: Rosekrans Hoffman: 5, 35, 46; Tom Leonard: 21–22, 43;
Sarah Snow: 24–25, 45; Troy Viss: 28, 40; Andrea Wallace: 4,
26

Photos: Courtesy American Antiquarian Society, *To the University
of Cambridge Manuscript by Phillis Wheatley:* 44; Library of
Congress, *Rules of Civility Manuscript Page by George Washington:*
44

Developed by Kirchoff/Wohlberg, Inc., in cooperation with Zaner-Bloser Publishers
Cover illustration by Sarah Snow

ISBN 0-88085-711-0

Copyright © 1996 Zaner-Bloser, Inc.

CONTENTS

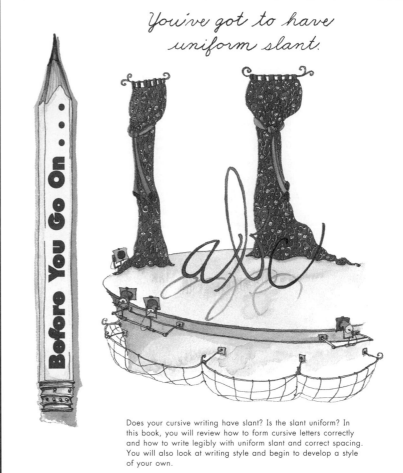

You've got to have uniform slant.

Before You Go On . . . .

Does your cursive writing have slant? Is the slant uniform? In this book, you will review how to form cursive letters correctly and how to write legibly with uniform slant and correct spacing. You will also look at writing style and begin to develop a style of your own.

4

UNIT SUMMARY

This page tells students about the content, organization, and focus of the book. Students begin by taking a pretest to assess current ability. The lessons that follow review what students need to know to develop good handwriting skills.

PREVIEW THE BOOK

Preview the book with students, calling attention to its organization.

- Unit 1 presents handwriting basics.
- Unit 2 introduces lowercase and uppercase cursive letters grouped by common strokes.
- Unit 3 provides a variety of opportunities for students to write independently and to develop a style of their own.

Point out that students will evaluate their handwriting frequently. Set up a portfolio for each student to assess individual progress throughout the year.

Have You Ever Seen?

Have you ever seen a sheet on a river bed?
Or a single hair from a hammer's head?
Has the foot of a mountain any toes?
And is there a pair of garden hose?

Does the needle ever wink its eye?
Why doesn't the wing of a building fly?
Can you tickle the ribs of a parasol?
Or open the trunk of a tree at all?

Are the teeth of a rake ever going to bite?
Have the hands of a clock any left or right?
Can the garden plot be deep and dark?
And what is the sound of the birch's bark?

On your paper, write the first stanza of this poem in your best cursive handwriting.

EVALUATE

Are all your tall letters the same height?	Yes	No
Are your short letters half the height of your tall letters?	Yes	No
Did you avoid collisions?	Yes	No
Does your writing have uniform slant?	Yes	No
Is your spacing correct?	Yes	No

5

EVALUATE

As students write, monitor and informally assess their performance. Then guide them through the self-evaluation process. Meet individually with students to help them assess their handwriting. Ask them how they would like to improve their writing. (visual, auditory)

PRETEST
Have students use the first stanza of the poem as a model for writing. Remind them to use correct letter size and shape, uniform slant, and correct spacing as they write. Tell students to place their pretests in their writing portfolios so they can write the same selection for the posttest later in the year. (visual, auditory, kinesthetic)

COACHING HINT: SELF-EVALUATION

Self-evaluation is an important step in the handwriting process. By identifying their own strengths and weaknesses, students become independent learners. The steps in the self-evaluation process are as follows:

1. Question
Students should ask themselves questions such as these: "Is my slant correct?" "Do my letters rest on the baseline?"

2. Compare
Students should compare their handwriting to correct models.

3. Evaluate
Students should determine strengths and weaknesses in their handwriting based on the keys to legibility.

4. Diagnose
Students should diagnose the cause of any difficulties. Possible causes include incorrect paper or pencil position, inconsistent pressure on pencil, and incorrect strokes.

5. Improve
Self-evaluation should include a means of improvement through additional instruction and continued practice. (visual, auditory, kinesthetic)

IMPORTANT STROKES FOR CURSIVE WRITING

UNDERCURVE
Curve under and up.

UNDERCURVE
Curve under and up.

DOWNCURVE
Curve left and down.

DOWNCURVE
Curve left and down.

OVERCURVE
Curve up and right.

OVERCURVE
Curve up and right.

SLANT
Slant left.

SLANT
Slant left.

Writing Positions and Important Strokes

Sit properly and hold your pencil correctly.

If you are left-handed . . .

Slant your paper with the lower right corner pointing toward you.

If you are right-handed . . .

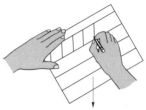

Slant your paper with the lower left corner pointing toward you.

Practice the strokes.

Undercurve

Downcurve

Overcurve

Slant

Undercurves swing.
Downcurves dive.
Overcurves bounce.
Slants just slide.

Undercurve, downcurve.
Overcurve, slant.
As you write cursive letters,
Remember this chant.

6

MODEL THE WRITING

Demonstrate correct positions for both left-handed and right-handed writers. Then model the two sizes of each stroke on guidelines. Invite students to say the names as they write the strokes. (visual, auditory, kinesthetic)

EVALUATE

As students write, check for correct paper and pencil positions. The Zaner-Bloser Writing Frame can be used to improve hand position. (visual, kinesthetic)

Cursive Letters and Numerals

Aa Bb Cc Dd Ee Ff Gg
Hh Ii Jj Kk Ll Mm
Nn Oo Pp Qq Rr Ss Tt
Uu Vv Ww Xx Yy Zz
1 2 3 4 5 6 7 8 9 10

Write some letters that have undercurves ⟋.
_____

Write some letters that have downcurves ⟨.
_____

Write some letters that have overcurves ⟨.
_____

Write some numerals that have slant strokes ⟋.
_____

Write the letters and numerals you want to improve.
_____
_____
_____

7

EVALUATE
Poll students to find out which letters and numerals are most difficult for them to write. Discuss how students can correct the problems they identify. (auditory)

CURSIVE LETTERS AND NUMERALS
Students can use the chart at the top of the page to review cursive letters and numerals. (visual, auditory)

COACHING HINT
Review with students the use of guidelines for correct letter formation. Draw guidelines on the chalkboard, and invite volunteers to write words on the guidelines. (visual, auditory, kinesthetic)

COACHING HINT: USE OF THE CHALKBOARD
You and your students can follow these suggestions for writing on the chalkboard.

Left-Hander. Stand in front of the writing lines and pull the downstrokes to the left elbow. The elbow is bent, and the writing is done at a comfortable height. Step to the right often to maintain correct slant.

Right-Hander. Stand to the left of the writing lines and pull the downstrokes toward the midsection of the body. The elbow is bent, and the writing is done at a comfortable height. Step to the right often to maintain correct slant. (visual, kinesthetic)

UNIT SUMMARY

This lesson serves as an introduction to Unit 2. The lessons that follow emphasize cursive letter formation and joinings. The Teacher Edition includes information on optional joinings of uppercase letters. Evaluations focus on letter size and shape.

PREVIEW THE UNIT

Preview the unit with students, calling attention to these features:

- letter models with numbered directional arrows
- guidelines for student writing directly beneath handwriting models
- reminders about joining letters
- geographical facts
- independent writing activities
- opportunities to evaluate letter size and shape

COACHING HINT

Demonstrate for students the technique of drawing a horizontal line with a ruler along the tops of their letters to show proper size. Have them practice this technique periodically to evaluate their letter size in curriculum areas that require handwriting, especially those that involve writing sentences or paragraphs. (visual, auditory, kinesthetic)

Keys to Legibility

To help make your writing legible, pay attention to size and shape, slant, and spacing.

Size and Shape

Tall letters should not touch the headline.

Some lowercase letters are tall letters.

d h l

All uppercase letters are tall letters.

X Y Z

Numerals are the height of tall letters.

0 9 8

Short letters should be half the height of tall letters.

Some lowercase letters are short letters.

c g m

Descenders should not go too far below the baseline.

Some lowercase letters have descenders.

Some uppercase letters have descenders.

g p q

J Y Z

Write the words beneath the models. Pay careful attention to the size and shape of your letters.

undercurve   downcurve

overcurve   slant

EVALUATE Compare your words with the models.
Are your letters the same size and shape?   Yes   No

8

MODEL THE WRITING

Model writing a tall letter, a short letter, and a letter with a descender, noting the placement of each letter on the guidelines. Remind students that all letters of the same size should be the same height. (visual, auditory)

EVALUATE

Guide students through the self-evaluation process. Then ask if they can read their words easily. Encourage them to explain why or why not. (visual, auditory)

Slant

The slant of your writing should be uniform.

All your letters should slant forward.

(handwriting sample)

Check the slant. Draw lines through the slant strokes of the letters.

Are your lines parallel?

Spacing

Your spacing should be correct.

between letters

between words

between sentences

letters

word word

end O Begin

Check the spacing. Draw O between letters, \ between words,

and O between sentences. Then write the sentences.

This spacing is correct. Shift your paper as you write.

Write this sentence. Pay careful attention to slant and spacing.

This is my best handwriting.

EVALUATE Does your writing have uniform slant?   Yes   No

Is your spacing correct?   Yes   No

9

PRACTICE MASTERS FOR UNIT 2

- Letters, 1–11
- Certificates, 14–16
- Alphabet—English, 19
- Alphabet—Spanish, 20
- Stroke Descriptions—English, 21–23
- Stroke Descriptions—Spanish, 24–26
- Record of Student's Handwriting Skills, 13
- Zaner-Bloser Handwriting Grid, 54

COACHING HINT

You may wish to group left-handed students together for instruction, if you can do so without calling attention to the practice. They should be seated to the left of the chalkboard.

MODEL THE WRITING

To show an example of correct slant and spacing, write the following sentences on guidelines: *My writing is legible. The slant and the spacing are correct.* Invite students to check the slant by drawing lines through the slant strokes in the letters and to check the spacing by drawing ovals between letters, by drawing slanted lines between words, and by writing uppercase **O** between sentences. (visual, auditory, kinesthetic)

EVALUATE

Guide students through the self-evaluation process. Then ask them if they can read their sentences easily. Encourage them to explain why or why not. (visual, auditory)

Undercurve
Slant, undercurve, (lift)
Dot

Undercurve
Slant, undercurve, (lift)
Slide right

Undercurve
Slant, undercurve
Slant, undercurve

Undercurve
Slant, undercurve
Slant, undercurve
Checkstroke

Write Undercurve Letters

Write the letters, joinings, and words.

i   i   i   i   is   id   in

issue   accident   inheritance

t   t   t   t   te   ta   ty

terrier   tactful   authority

u   u   u   u   up   uc   um

uproar   success   autumn

CHECKSTROKE ALERT

w   w   w   w   wi   wa   wn

withhold   renewable   thrown

EVALUATE   Circle your best joining.
Circle your best word.

10

PRACTICE MASTER I

MODEL THE WRITING

Model each letter and say the stroke descriptions, emphasizing the beginning undercurve stroke in each. Ask questions such as these:
In what ways are the letters alike?
Which letter ends with a checkstroke?
Which letters have a lift?
How is **w** different from **u**?
(visual, auditory)

EVALUATE

To help students evaluate their writing, ask questions such as these:
Did you pull the slant strokes to the baseline?
Are the slant strokes in **u** and **w** parallel?
Do all your letters rest on the baseline?
(visual, auditory)

Write Undercurve Letters

Write the letters, joinings, and words.

r   r   r   rh   ro   ry

rhythm   roommate   necessary

s   s   s   se   sc   sy

security   mischief   synthetic

p   p   p   pr   po   py

prospect   poncho   pyramid

j   j   j   je   ja   jo

jealous   life jacket   enjoyable

EVALUATE Circle your best joining.
Circle your best word.

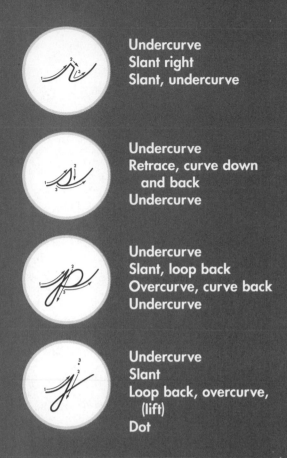

Undercurve
Slant right
Slant, undercurve

Undercurve
Retrace, curve down
  and back
Undercurve

Undercurve
Slant, loop back
Overcurve, curve back
Undercurve

Undercurve
Slant
Loop back, overcurve,
  (lift)
Dot

MODEL THE WRITING

Model each letter and say the stroke descriptions, emphasizing the beginning undercurve stroke in each. Ask questions such as these:
How do all the letters begin?
Which letters have descenders?
Which letter ends with an overcurve?
How do the other letters end?
(visual, auditory)

EVALUATE

To help students evaluate their writing, ask questions such as these:
Does your **r** have correct slant?
Do the loops of your **p** and **j** close at the baseline?
(visual, auditory)

Name

Write the letters, joinings, and words.

r r r re ra rm

residue adorable permission

s s s su sq sm

submarine mosque cytoplasm

p p p pe pa py

perspire partner papyrus

j j j ju jo ja

broad jump jovial jagged

EVALUATE Circle your best joining.
Circle your best word.

PRACTICE MASTER 2

PRACTICE MASTER 2

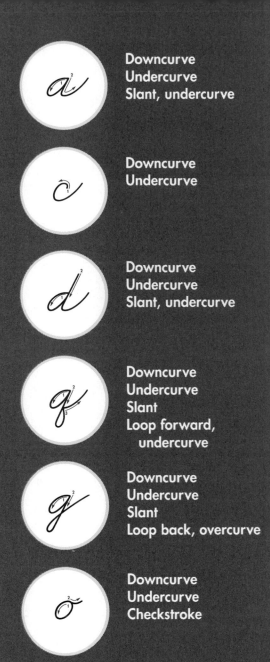

a
Downcurve
Undercurve
Slant, undercurve

c
Downcurve
Undercurve

d
Downcurve
Undercurve
Slant, undercurve

q
Downcurve
Undercurve
Slant
Loop forward,
  undercurve

g
Downcurve
Undercurve
Slant
Loop back, overcurve

o
Downcurve
Undercurve
Checkstroke

Name

Write the letters, joinings, and words.

a a a   c c c
al ac an   ce ca cn
announce   carriage
d d d   q q q
dr do dm   qu qu qu
dreadful   quarterback
g g g   **CHECKSTROKE ALERT**
ge ga gy   o o o
geologist   ol og ov
                 overhead

EVALUATE Circle your best joining.
Circle your best word.

PRACTICE MASTER 3

PRACTICE MASTER 3

12

Write Downcurve Letters

Write the letters, joinings, and words.

a   a   a   a   **c**   c   c   c
ap   ad   az   cl   co   cy
appreciate   classify

d   d   d   d   **q**   q   q   q
dr   da   dy   qu   qu   qu
daydream   quotation

g   g   g   g   **CHECKSTROKE ALERT**
gr   go   gn   **o**   o   o   o
good-natured   oi   oc   on
                           occasion

EVALUATE Circle your best joining.
Circle your best word.

12

MODEL THE WRITING

Model each letter and say the stroke descriptions, emphasizing the downcurve stroke in each. Ask questions such as these:
How are **a** and **d** alike?
How does **g** differ from **q**?
How are **o** and **c** alike?
How does **o** end?
(visual, auditory)

EVALUATE

To help students evaluate their writing, ask questions such as these:
Do all your letters have correct slant?
Did you pull the slant strokes in **a** and **d** to the baseline?
Do the loops of your **q** and **g** close at the baseline?
(visual, auditory)

Write Overcurve Letters

Write the letters, joinings, and words.

ⓜ *n n n* ⓜ *m m m*

ni ng nn   *mu mo mm*

beginning   *mosquito*

ⓧ *x x x*   ⓨ *y y y*

xp xa xy   *ye yo yy*

experiment   *beyond*

ⓩ *z z z*   ⓥ **CHECKSTROKE ALERT**

zi zo zy   *v v v*

zygote   *vi va vy*

victory

Circle your best joining.
Circle your best word.

13

ⓜ	Overcurve, slant Overcurve, slant Undercurve
ⓜ	Overcurve, slant Overcurve, slant Overcurve, slant Undercurve
ⓧ	Overcurve, slant Undercurve, (lift) Slant
ⓨ	Overcurve, slant Undercurve Slant Loop back, overcurve
ⓩ	Overcurve, slant Overcurve Curve down Loop, overcurve
ⓥ	Overcurve, slant Undercurve Checkstroke

MODEL THE WRITING

Model each letter and say the stroke descriptions, emphasizing the beginning overcurve stroke in each. Ask questions such as these:
How do all the letters begin?
Which letters end with an overcurve?
Which letter has a lift?
(visual, auditory)

EVALUATE

To help students evaluate their writing, ask questions such as these:
Is your **x** crossed in the middle of the slant stroke?
Does your **v** end with a checkstroke?
Is each letter about the same width as the model?
(visual, auditory)

Name

Write the letters, joinings, and words.

n n n   *m m m*

ne nd ny   *mu ma my*

nervous   *mirror*

x x x   *y y y*

xt xc xy   *ys ya ym*

excess   *ecosystem*

z z z   **CHECKSTROKE ALERT**

ze za zy   *v v v*

criticize   *ve vo vy*

volume

Circle your best joining.
Circle your best word.

Copyright © Zaner-Bloser, Inc.   **PRACTICE MASTER 4**

PRACTICE MASTER 4

13

**Undercurve
Loop back, slant
Undercurve**

**Undercurve
Loop back, slant
Undercurve**

**Undercurve
Loop back, slant
Overcurve, slant
Undercurve**

**Undercurve
Loop back, slant
Overcurve, curve
    forward, curve under
Slant right, undercurve**

**Undercurve
Loop back, slant
Loop forward
Undercurve**

**Undercurve
Loop back, slant
Undercurve
Checkstroke**

Write Letters With Loops

Write the letters, joinings, and words.

e e e e
ef ea em
emotion

l l l l
li lo ly
lieutenant

h h h h
he ha hy
handkerchief

k k k k
kl ko kn
knowledge

f f f f
fi fa fy
fierce

CHECKSTROKE ALERT

b b b b
br ba by
brochure

EVALUATE Circle your best joining.
Circle your best word.

14

PRACTICE MASTER 5

14

MODEL THE WRITING

Model each letter and say the stroke descriptions, emphasizing the beginning loop in each. Ask questions such as these:
In what ways are the letters alike?
Which letters end with an undercurve?
How does **b** end?
(visual, auditory)

EVALUATE

To help students evaluate their writing, ask questions such as these:
Are all your letters the correct size?
Is the forward curve of your **k** closed?
Does the lower loop of your **f** close at the baseline?
(visual, auditory)

Legible Letters

Follow these suggestions to avoid common handwriting errors and to form legible letters.

Do not loop non-looped letters. Write *u*, not *ee*.

Keep loops open in letters with loops. Write *l*, not *l*.

Close letters that should be closed. Write *d*, not *d*.

Form curves carefully. Write *n*, not *n*.

Can you read these words? Take your best guess and write each word.

actual	*neighbor*
carefully	*distance*
beliefs	*acid*

On Your Own Choose eight spelling words or words from your reading and writing, and write them. Form your letters carefully.

EVALUATE

Is each *t* made without a loop?	Yes	No
Is the loop in each *l* open?	Yes	No
Did you close each *a* ?	Yes	No
Did you close each *d* ?	Yes	No
Did you form each *n* correctly?	Yes	No

15

EVALUATE

Guide students through the self-evaluation process. Then ask if they can read their words easily. Encourage them to explain why or why not. (visual, auditory)

BEFORE WRITING

Talk about problems caused by poor handwriting. Poll students to find out how many have lost credit on spelling tests because words appeared to be misspelled. Remind students of the importance of writing legibly so they and others can read what they write.

COACHING HINT

Keep a record of the letters students are having problems with. Provide practice with these letters by assigning writing exercises such as making word lists and writing tongue twisters. (visual, auditory, kinesthetic)

KEYS TO LEGIBILITY: SIZE AND SHAPE

Discuss how the lowercase letters are grouped. Draw attention to the ending stroke of each letter. Model how to join the letter to

- an undercurve
- a downcurve
- an overcurve

Provide opportunities for students to practice the joinings on handwriting guidelines. (visual, auditory, kinesthetic)

COACHING HINT

The joining stroke between letters must be wide enough to allow for good spacing. There should be just enough space for a minimum-sized oval. Have students practice joinings to reinforce both fluent strokes and good spacing. (visual, kinesthetic)

Review

Write each joining. Then write a word using the joining.

undercurve to undercurve	*lu*
undercurve to downcurve	*ro*
undercurve to overcurve	*ex*
overcurve to undercurve	*ye*
overcurve to downcurve	*ja*
overcurve to overcurve	*zy*
checkstroke to undercurve	*wi*
checkstroke to downcurve	*ba*
checkstroke to overcurve	*om*

Write a paragraph using some of the words you wrote above.

EVALUATE Circle your best joining.
Circle your best word.

16

EVALUATE

Guide students through the self-evaluation process, focusing on joinings. Encourage them to explain why one joining or word they wrote might be better than another. (visual, auditory)

Certificates of Progress *should be awarded to those students who show notable handwriting progress and* Certificates of Excellence *to those who progress to the top levels of handwriting proficiency.*

Write Downcurve Letters

$\mathcal{A}$, $\mathcal{C}$, and $\mathcal{E}$ are joined to the letter that follows.
$\mathcal{O}$ is not joined to the letter that follows.

Write the letters, joinings, and words. Then write the sentence.

$\mathcal{A}$ $\mathcal{A}$ $\mathcal{A}$ $\mathcal{A}$ As Ac An

$Asia$ $Acadia$ $Ankara$

$\mathcal{C}$ $\mathcal{C}$ $\mathcal{C}$ Cu Ca Cy

$Cuba$ $Cairo$ $Cyclades$

$\mathcal{E}$ $\mathcal{E}$ $\mathcal{E}$ Eu Eg Ex

$Eurasia$ $Egypt$ $Exmoor$

$\mathcal{O}$ $\mathcal{O}$ $\mathcal{O}$ $Oslo$ $Oman$

DID YOU KNOW?

Oman has four official languages.

EVALUATE Circle your best word.

17

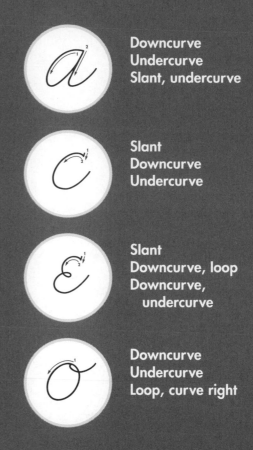

Downcurve
Undercurve
Slant, undercurve

Slant
Downcurve
Undercurve

Slant
Downcurve, loop
Downcurve,
 undercurve

Downcurve
Undercurve
Loop, curve right

MODEL THE WRITING

Model each letter and say the stroke descriptions, emphasizing the downcurve stroke in each. Ask questions such as these:
Which letters begin with a downcurve?
Which letters begin with slant, downcurve?
Where is the loop in **O**?
(visual, auditory)

EVALUATE

To help students evaluate their writing, ask questions such as these:
Are all your letters the correct size?
Do your letters have correct slant?
Did you close your **A** and your **O**?
(visual, auditory)

PRACTICE MASTER 6

17

Curve forward, slant
Overcurve, slant
Undercurve

Curve forward, slant
Overcurve, slant
Overcurve, slant
Undercurve

Curve forward, slant,
(lift)
Doublecurve
Curve forward,
  undercurve

Curve forward, slant,
(lift)
Curve back, slant
Retrace, loop, curve
right

Write Curve Forward Letters

n, m, K, and *H* are joined to the letter that follows.

Write the letters, joinings, and words.

n   n   n   ne   na   no

Nepal   Nablus   Northumberland

m   m   m   me   ma   my

Meerut   Madrid   Mysore

K   K   K   Ke   Ko   Ky

Kenya   Kodiak   Kyushu

H   H   H   Hu   Ho   Hy

Hungary   Hobart   Hyrcania

EVALUATE Circle your best word.

18

PRACTICE MASTER 7

18

MODEL THE WRITING

Model each letter and say the stroke descriptions, emphasizing the curve forward, slant strokes in each. Ask questions such as these:
How are **H** and **K** alike?
How does **N** differ from **M**?
How many slant strokes does each letter have?
(visual, auditory)

EVALUATE

To help students evaluate their writing, ask questions such as these:
Are your slant strokes parallel?
Is each letter about the same width as the model?
Is the second overcurve in your **M** shorter than the first?
(visual, auditory)

Write Curve Forward Letters

$\mathcal{U}$, $\mathcal{Y}$, and $\mathcal{Z}$ are joined to the letter that follows.
$\mathcal{V}$, $\mathcal{X}$, and $\mathcal{W}$ are not joined to the letter that follows.

Write the letters, joinings, and words.

$\mathcal{U}$ $\mathcal{U}$ $\mathcal{U}$ $\mathcal{U}$ $\mathcal{Ur}$ $\mathcal{Ug}$ $\mathcal{Ux}$

$\mathcal{Y}$ $\mathcal{Ur}$ *Uganda*   *Uxbridge*

$\mathcal{Y}$ $\mathcal{Y}$ $\mathcal{Y}$ *Ye*   *Ya*   *Yo*

$\mathcal{Z}$ *Yerevan*   *Yarmouth*   *Yokohama*

   $\mathcal{Z}$ $\mathcal{Z}$ $\mathcal{Z}$ *Zu*   *Ze*   *Za*

$\mathcal{V}$ *Zug*   *New Zealand*   *Zaire*

$\mathcal{X}$ $\mathcal{V}$ $\mathcal{V}$ $\mathcal{V}$ *Venice*   *Vancouver*

   $\mathcal{X}$ $\mathcal{X}$ $\mathcal{X}$ *Xinjiang*   *Xuzhou*

$\mathcal{W}$ $\mathcal{W}$ $\mathcal{W}$ $\mathcal{W}$ *West Indies*   *Wales*

EVALUATE Circle your best word.

19

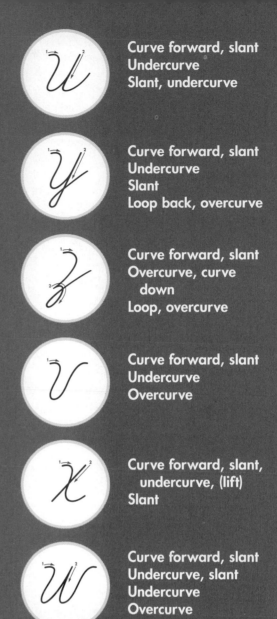

Curve forward, slant
Undercurve
Slant, undercurve

Curve forward, slant
Undercurve
Slant
Loop back, overcurve

Curve forward, slant
Overcurve, curve down
Loop, overcurve

Curve forward, slant
Undercurve
Overcurve

Curve forward, slant, undercurve, (lift)
Slant

Curve forward, slant
Undercurve, slant
Undercurve
Overcurve

MODEL THE WRITING

Model each letter and say the stroke descriptions, emphasizing the curve forward, slant strokes in each. Ask questions such as these:
How do all the letters begin?
Which letters end with an overcurve?
Which letter has a lift?
(visual, auditory)

EVALUATE

To help students evaluate their writing, ask questions such as these:
Did you pull the slant strokes in **U** to the baseline?
Do the loops of your **Y** and **Z** close at the baseline?
Is each letter about the same width as the model?
(visual, auditory)

Joining Alert

Joining **X** to the letter that follows is optional.

PRACTICE MASTER 8

19

Slant, curve forward
and right, (lift)
Doublecurve, curve up
Retrace, curve right

Slant, curve forward
and right, (lift)
Doublecurve, curve up
Retrace, curve right,
   (lift)
Slide right

Overcurve
Curve down and up
Retrace, curve right

Curve back, overcurve
Curve down, retrace
Curve forward, curve
   under

Overcurve
Slant
Loop back, overcurve

Write Doublecurve and Overcurve Letters

T, F, I, and *Q* are not joined to the letter that follows.
J is joined to the letter that follows.

Write the letters, joinings, and words. Then write the sentences.

T   T   T   Tibet   Tonga

F   F   F   Fiji   Falkland Islands

I   I   I   Italy   India

Q   Q   Q   Quebec   Quito

J   J   J   Ju   Ja   Jo

San Juan   Japan   Jordan

DID YOU KNOW?

Tonga is part of Polynesia.

Fiji is part of Melanesia.

EVALUATE Circle your best word.

20

PRACTICE MASTER 9

20

MODEL THE WRITING

Model each letter and say the stroke descriptions, emphasizing the doublecurve in **T** and **F** and the overcurve in **I, J,** and **Q**. Ask students questions such as these:
Which letters have a doublecurve?
Which letters have an overcurve?
Which letters have a lift?
(visual, auditory)

EVALUATE

To help students evaluate their writing, ask questions such as these:
Does your **F** have a slide right stroke?
Do the loops of your **J** close at the baseline?
Does your **Q** end below the baseline?
(visual, auditory)

Joining Alert
Joining **T, F,** and **I** to the letter that follows is optional.

Write Letters With Loops

G, S, L, and *D* are not joined to the letter that follows.

Write the letters and words. Then write the sentences.

G   G   G   Greece   Gobi Desert

S   S   S   Spain   Salzburg

L   L   L   Lebanon   Latvia

D   D   D   Denmark   Djibouti

DID YOU KNOW?

Greece's flag has a white cross.

There is a crest on Spain's flag.

There is a tree on Lebanon's flag.

Djibouti's flag has a red star.

EVALUATE Circle your best word.

21

Undercurve, loop,
curve forward
Doublecurve, curve up
Retrace, curve right

Undercurve, loop
Curve down and up
Retrace, curve right

Undercurve
Loop, curve down
Loop, curve under

Doublecurve
Loop, curve down
  and up
Loop, curve right

MODEL THE WRITING

Model each letter and say the stroke descriptions, emphasizing the initial loop in each. Ask questions such as these:
Which letters begin at the baseline?
Which letters have a loop that rests on the baseline?
Which letter ends below the baseline?
(visual, auditory)

EVALUATE

To help students evaluate their writing, ask questions such as these:
Do all your letters have correct slant?
Is each letter about the same width as the model?
Does your **D** touch the baseline twice?
(visual, auditory)

Joining Alert

Joining **G** and **S** to the letter that follows is optional.

Name

G, S, L, and *D* are not joined to the letter that follows.

Write the letters and words. Then write the sentences.

G G G Ghana Gambia

S S S Senegal Somalia

L L L Liberia Laos

D D D Durban Dominica

DID YOU KNOW?

The cedi is Ghana's money.

Senegal uses the franc.

The kip is used in Laos.

Dominica uses a dollar.

EVALUATE Circle your best word.

Copyright © Zaner-Bloser, Inc.   **PRACTICE MASTER 10**

PRACTICE MASTER 10

**Undercurve, slant
Retrace, curve forward
and back**

**Undercurve, slant
Retrace, curve
forward, loop
Curve forward
and back
Retrace, curve right**

**Undercurve, slant
Retrace, curve forward
and back
Curve forward,
undercurve**

Write Undercurve-Slant Letters

$\mathcal{P}$ and $\mathcal{B}$ are not joined to the letter that follows.
$\mathcal{R}$ is joined to the letter that follows.

Write the letters, joinings, and words. Then write the sentences.

P   P   P   Peru   Pakistan

B   B   B   Bhutan   Bahrain

R   R   R   Rw   Ro   Ry

Rwanda   Romania   Ryukyu

DID YOU KNOW?

Pakistan's flag has a crescent moon.

Bhutan's flag has a white dragon.

The letter R is on Rwanda's flag.

EVALUATE Circle your best word.

22

Name

$\mathcal{P}$ and $\mathcal{B}$ are not joined to the letter that follows.
$\mathcal{R}$ is joined to the letter that follows.

Write the letters, joinings, and words. Then write the sentences.

P   P   P   Pisa   Paraguay

B   B   B   Belize   Bologna

R   R   R   Rw   Ro   Ry

Rimini   Rome   Ryazan

DID YOU KNOW?

Pisa has the Leaning Tower.

Bologna is famous for art.

The Colosseum is in Rome.

EVALUATE Circle your best word.

Copyright © Zaner-Bloser, Inc.   **PRACTICE MASTER II**

PRACTICE MASTER II

22

MODEL THE WRITING

Model each letter and say the stroke descriptions, emphasizing the undercurve-slant in each. Ask questions such as these:
Which letters curve forward and back to the slant stroke?
Which letter curves forward and loops?
How many retraces does each letter have?
(visual, auditory)

EVALUATE

To help students evaluate their writing, ask questions such as these:
Do your letters have correct slant?
Is each letter about the same width as the model?
Are the forward curves of your **B** parallel with the slant stroke?
(visual, auditory)

Joining Alert

Joining **B** to the letter that follows is optional.

Write Numerals

LEGIBLE LETTERS

Remember! Numerals are the same height as tall letters.

Write the numerals.

1 2 3 4 5 6 7 8 9 10

Palindromic numerals read the same backward and forward. One year in each century is a palindrome. Write these palindromic years.

1001 1111   1221 1331 1441
1551 1661 1771 1881 1991 2002

October 1, 1901, is a palindromic date. It can be written *10/1/01.*
At least one date in each decade is a palindrome. Write the cursive numerals for each palindromic date.

March 1, 1913 _____	July 2, 1927 _____
May 3, 1935 _____	February 4, 1942 _____
January 5, 1951 _____	April 6, 1964 _____
July 7, 1977 _____	September 8, 1989 _____
June 9, 1996 _____	October 11, 2001 _____
August 1, 2018 _____	December 22, 2021 _____

On Your Own Write the next palindromic date. _____

EVALUATE Are your numerals the correct height?   Yes   No

23

On the chalkboard, write the following words, sentence, and numerals:

- pop
- radar
- Madam, I'm Adam.
- 1991

Point out that these expressions are all palindromes: They read the same way forward and backward.

WRITE AWAY

Pair students and ask them to compile a list of word palindromes or to write their own sentence palindrome. Provide samples such as this for inspiration: *Able was I ere I saw Elba.*

COACHING HINT

Students' progress in handwriting is greater when short, intensive periods of instruction are used. Fifteen minutes for a lesson is optimal.

EVALUATE

Have students focus on size to determine whether their numerals are legible. Discuss ways to improve legibility. (visual, auditory)

BEFORE WRITING

Point out that every family, culture, and language has its own proverbs—short sayings based on experience or tradition. Discuss the meanings of such proverbs as "Birds of a feather flock together" and "Don't cry over spilled milk."

MANUSCRIPT MAINTENANCE

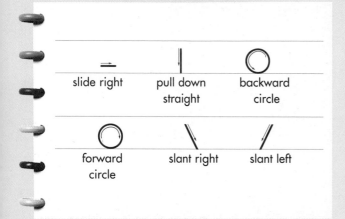

slide right   pull down straight   backward circle

forward circle   slant right   slant left

Review the basic strokes for manuscript writing. Remind students that all manuscript letters are formed with these strokes and that manuscript writing is vertical. Have them practice the strokes and letterforms. Tell them to adjust the position of the paper for manuscript writing. (visual, auditory, kinesthetic)

WRITE AWAY

Challenge students working in pairs to devise their own code and to write a proverb in code with a list of clues for decoding it. Students might use a familiar proverb or one they find listed in a collection of proverbs.

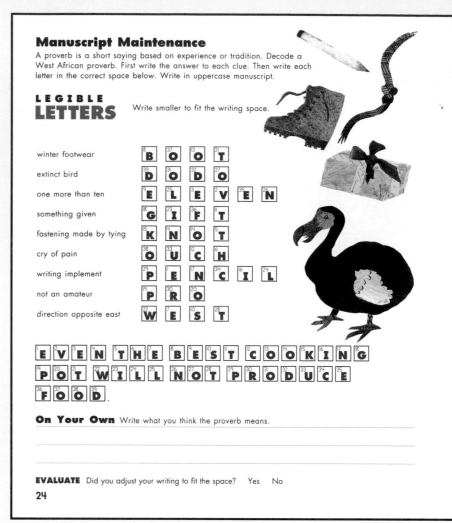

Manuscript Maintenance

A proverb is a short saying based on experience or tradition. Decode a West African proverb. First write the answer to each clue. Then write each letter in the correct space below. Write in uppercase manuscript.

LEGIBLE LETTERS   Write smaller to fit the writing space.

Clue	Answer
winter footwear	B O O T
extinct bird	D O D O
one more than ten	E L E V E N
something given	G I F T
fastening made by tying	K N O T
cry of pain	O U C H
writing implement	P E N C I L
not an amateur	P R O
direction opposite east	W E S T

EVEN THE BEST COOKING POT WILL NOT PRODUCE FOOD.

On Your Own Write what you think the proverb means.

_____

EVALUATE Did you adjust your writing to fit the space?   Yes   No

24

EVALUATE

Have students focus on size and shape to determine whether their uppercase manuscript letters are legible. Discuss ways to improve legibility. (visual, auditory)

Review

$\mathcal{A}, \mathcal{C}, \mathcal{E}, \mathcal{N}, \mathcal{M}, \mathcal{K}, \mathcal{H}, \mathcal{U}, \mathcal{Y}, \mathcal{Z}, \mathcal{I},$ and $\mathcal{R}$
are joined to the letter that follows.

$\mathcal{O}, \mathcal{V}, \mathcal{X}, \mathcal{W}, \mathcal{T}, \mathcal{F}, \mathcal{I}, \mathcal{Q}, \mathcal{G}, \mathcal{S}, \mathcal{L}, \mathcal{D}, \mathcal{P},$ and $\mathcal{B}$
are not joined to the letter that follows.

For each letter of the alphabet, write a place name.

$\mathcal{A}$ _____	$\mathcal{B}$ _____
$\mathcal{C}$ _____	$\mathcal{D}$ _____
$\mathcal{E}$ _____	$\mathcal{F}$ _____
$\mathcal{G}$ _____	$\mathcal{H}$ _____
$\mathcal{I}$ _____	$\mathcal{J}$ _____
$\mathcal{K}$ _____	$\mathcal{L}$ _____
$\mathcal{M}$ _____	$\mathcal{N}$ _____
$\mathcal{O}$ _____	$\mathcal{P}$ _____
$\mathcal{Q}$ _____	$\mathcal{R}$ _____
$\mathcal{S}$ _____	$\mathcal{T}$ _____
$\mathcal{U}$ _____	$\mathcal{V}$ _____
$\mathcal{W}$ _____	$\mathcal{X}$ _____
$\mathcal{Y}$ _____	$\mathcal{Z}$ _____

EVALUATE Circle your best word.

 DID YOU KNOW There are more than 180 countries in the world.

25

EVALUATE

Guide students through the self-evaluation process, focusing on joinings. Encourage them to explain why one joining or word they wrote might be better than another. (visual, auditory)

Certificates of Progress *should be awarded to those students who show notable handwriting progress and* Certificates of Excellence *to those who progress to the top levels of handwriting proficiency.*

KEYS TO LEGIBILITY: SIZE AND SHAPE

Discuss how the uppercase letters are grouped. Draw attention to the ending stroke of each letter. Point out the letters that are joined to the letter that follows. Model how to join a letter to

- an undercurve
- a downcurve
- an overcurve

Provide opportunities for students to practice the joinings. (visual, auditory, kinesthetic)

COACHING HINT

On the chalkboard, write words with several obvious errors in the formation of letters. Have students come to the chalkboard to locate, identify, and correct the errors. (visual, kinesthetic)

WRITE AWAY

Ask students to choose a place name they wrote on page 25 and to write a story explaining how the place got its name. Students can provide either an imaginative or a factual explanation.

In the following lessons, you will write more and look closely at your handwriting. You will focus on size and shape, slant, and spacing to help you develop a legible personal style. Write your signature to show your personal style.

UNIT SUMMARY

This page serves as an introduction to Unit 3. The unit is divided into two sections, each having a different handwriting emphasis: (1) size and shape and (2) slant and spacing. The lessons in each section provide opportunities for meaningful practice and application of handwriting skills in a variety of formats. Evaluations focus on the keys to legibility. The primary goal is for students to develop a legible personal style of cursive writing.

PREVIEW THE UNIT

Preview the unit with students, calling attention to these features:
• timed writing exercises
• lessons on developing personal style
• everyday writing applications
• proofreading practice
• creative writing assignments
• writing in other languages
• manuscript maintenance

Also call attention to these page features:
• writing models
• hints for writing legibly
• writing extensions
• opportunities to evaluate legibility
• facts about people, places, and things

Keys to Legibility: Size and Shape

LEGIBLE LETTERS

Remember! Tall letters should not touch the headline. Short letters should be half the height of tall letters. Descenders should not go too far below the baseline.

Aa   Bb   Cc   Dd   Ee   Ff   Gg
Hh   Ii   Jj   Kk   Ll   Mm
Nn   Oo   Pp   Qq   Rr   Ss   Tt
Uu   Vv   Ww   Xx   Yy   Zz
1   2   3   4   5   6   7   8   9   10

Write the uppercase letters.

_____

_____

Write the tall lowercase letters.

_____

Write the short lowercase letters.

_____

Write the letters with descenders.

_____

Write the numerals *1* through *10.*

EVALUATE   Are all your tall letters the same height?   Yes   No
Are all your short letters the same height?   Yes   No
Are your numerals the same height as tall letters? Yes   No

27

MODEL THE WRITING

Model writing a tall letter, a short letter, and a letter with a descender, noting the placement of each letter on the guidelines. Remind students that all letters of the same size should be the same height. (visual, auditory)

EVALUATE

Guide students through the self-evaluation process. Then ask if they can read their letters and numerals easily. Encourage them to explain why or why not. (visual, auditory)

PRACTICE MASTERS FOR UNIT 3

- Manuscript Maintenance, 12
- Certificates, 14–16
- Write in Spanish, 27–45
- Write in the Content Areas, 46–53
- Record of Student's Handwriting Skills, 13
- Zaner-Bloser Handwriting Grid, 54

BEFORE WRITING

Tell students they will be completing a timed writing exercise to find out how quickly and legibly they can write in cursive. Point out that they will be writing a pangram—a sentence that includes all 26 letters of the alphabet. Students may wish to check that all 26 letters appear in the model sentence.

KEYS TO LEGIBILITY: SIZE AND SHAPE

Remind students that all letters of the same size should be even in height and that descenders should not go too far below the baseline. Point out that smooth handwriting is a result of *writing* letters, not drawing them. Provide opportunities to practice letters and joinings on guidelines. (visual, auditory, kinesthetic)

WRITE AWAY

Share with students several additional pangrams, such as "The five boxing wizards jump quickly" and "Quick waxy bugs jump the frozen veldt." Ask them to write a sentence using as many different letters as they can. Suggest they use words such as *vex, quick, vie,* and *waltz* in their sentences.

Write Quickly

Practice writing quickly. Write this alphabet sentence as many times as you can in one minute. At the same time, try to write legibly.

The quick brown fox jumps over the lazy dog.

LEGIBLE LETTERS Do not draw your letters. Write smoothly.

_____

_____

_____

_____

_____

_____

_____

_____

_____

_____

EVALUATE Can you read your writing easily?   Yes   No
Can a friend read it?   Yes   No

DID YOU KNOW?   An alphabet sentence, or pangram, uses all 26 letters of the alphabet.

28

EVALUATE

Help students determine whether writing quickly has affected the size and shape of their letters. Suggest they choose a word that needs improvement. Encourage them to practice the letters and joinings in that word. (visual, auditory)

Personal Style

You and your classmates have learned how to write Zaner-Bloser cursive letters. Yet no one's handwriting is exactly like yours. As you write, you develop a personal style that is yours alone.

Check the items that tell about your personal style of writing.

☐ *I like to write small.*

☐ *I like to write big.*

☐ *I like to make fancy letters.*

☐ Other. Describe: _____

_____

_____

LEGIBLE LETTERS

Personal differences are acceptable as long as your handwriting is legible.

Use your own style to write your favorite saying.

_____

_____

_____

What do you think your handwriting shows about you?

_____

_____

EVALUATE Ask a friend to read and evaluate your writing.
Is it legible?   Yes   No

DID YOU KNOW Graphology is the study of the relationship between handwriting and personality.

29

EVALUATE

Pair students and have them discuss their personal handwriting styles. Encourage students to experiment with different handwriting styles, reminding them to keep their writing legible. (visual, auditory, kinesthetic)

BEFORE WRITING

Have several volunteers write their signatures on the chalkboard. Compare the way they form their letters. Discuss what makes each person's signature unique. Point out that all writers personalize their handwriting in some way. Larger or smaller letters and simpler or more elaborate letters are acceptable as long as the writing is still legible.

WRITE AWAY

Ask students to find a copy of a signature of a famous person in an encyclopedia or a book of autographs. Have students write a brief description of how the person personalized his or her signature.

COACHING HINT

Correct body position influences smoothness. Encourage students to sit comfortably erect, with their feet flat on the floor and their hips touching the back of the chair. Both arms should rest on the desk. The elbows should be off the desk. (kinesthetic)

BEFORE WRITING

Discuss family names with students. Ask if any students know the meaning of their family names. You may wish to share with students the meaning of your family name.

KEYS TO LEGIBILITY: SIZE AND SHAPE

Remind students to shift words with ascenders so they do not collide with descenders above them. Provide practice in writing tall letters below letters with descenders. (visual, auditory, kinesthetic)

WRITE AWAY

Write the following family names and their meanings on the chalkboard:

- Glenn—small valley
- Michaelson—son of Michael
- Keating—cheerful person
- Foss—waterfall
- Rizzo —curly-haired person
- Harper—harp player
- Hodgkins—son of young Roger

Ask students to add these names or others to their outlines.

Write an Outline

An outline is a writing plan. Here is the first part of an outline for a report on family names.

What's in a Name? ← title
I. *History of Family Names* ← main topic
    A. *Beginnings* ← subtopic
       1. Chinese—first to have more than one name ← detail
       2. Roman Empire—used three names
    B. *Middle Ages*

Use the details listed below to complete the second part of the outline. As you write, pay attention to the size and shape of your letters.

Yamashita—below the mountain   *Barker—shepherd*
Chandler—candlemaker   *Bach—lives by the brook*

II. *Sources of Family Names*
    A. *Father's name*
       1. Karlsdotter—daughter of Karl
       2. Ben-David—son of David
    B. *Occupational names*

      1. _____
      2. _____
    C. *Place names*

      1. _____
      2. _____

EVALUATE Are your short letters half the height of your tall letters?   Yes No

30

EVALUATE

After students have evaluated the size of their letters, ask if their writing is legible. Have them explain why or why not. (visual, auditory)

Write a Paragraph

The following sentences tell about different customs for naming children. Put the sentences in a paragraph by adding a topic sentence. Write the complete paragraph.

Many African children receive one name at birth and a second name later on. In China, names for boys are often plain, while names for girls are elaborate. Greek parents traditionally name the firstborn child after a paternal grandparent.

COLLISION ALERT   Make sure your tall letters do not bump into the descenders above them.

_____

_____

_____

_____

_____

_____

_____

_____

_____

EVALUATE   Did you avoid collisions?   Yes   No

Is your writing legible?   Yes   No

31

EVALUATE

After students have evaluated the legibility of their writing, discuss "bumping." Ask what they did to avoid collisions. Encourage students to practice writing words with tall letters beneath words with descenders, shifting words slightly if necessary. (visual, auditory, kinesthetic)

BEFORE WRITING

Discuss first names with students. Point out that parents have many different reasons for choosing a child's name. They may choose a name that describes a quality they want the child to have. They may choose a name to impart a certain feeling. They may follow certain ethnic or religious customs. They may name the child after a friend or relative.

WRITE AWAY

Ask students to write a paragraph about their first name. They can tell why they received it, what it means, and whether or not they like it. If they prefer, they might write a paragraph about a name they would have chosen for themselves.

Practice Masters 46–53 provide practice in writing across the curriculum.

COACHING HINT

On the chalkboard, demonstrate the letters with descenders. Have students trace the descending stroke with colored chalk to highlight its shape and size. (visual, kinesthetic)

BEFORE WRITING

Review the role of editing and the use of proofreading marks in the writing process. On the chalkboard write several sentences with various errors. Demonstrate how to use the proofreading marks to mark the errors.

KEYS TO LEGIBILITY: SIZE AND SHAPE

Remind students that tall letters should not touch the headline, short letters should be half the height of tall letters, and descenders should not go too far below the baseline. (visual)

WRITE AWAY

Ask students to write a paragraph about their hometown and then use the proofreading marks shown on page 32 to edit it. Students may then write their corrected paragraph in their best handwriting.

Edit Your Writing

Use these proofreading marks to edit your writing.

≡ Capitalize.   ∧ Insert (add).

/ Use lowercase.   ⌒ Delete (take out).

⊙ Add period.   ¶ Indent for paragraph.

Write this paragraph. Make the changes indicated by the proofreading marks.

¶ Limerick is the ∧third largest city of the Republic of Ireland. ∧A limerick It is also a ~~kinds~~ form of ~~silly poetry~~ humorous verse⊙ which came first. The city or the verse? The verse ∧probably gets its name from an ∧old Irish song⊙ "Will You Come Up To Limerick?"

_____

_____

_____

_____

_____

_____

_____

EVALUATE Ask a friend to proofread your writing. Is the paragraph written correctly?   Yes   No

32

EVALUATE

After students have proofread their paragraphs, ask if they are legible. Ask them to explain why or why not. (visual, auditory)

Manuscript Maintenance

To request a book at the library, fill out the call slip below. Use the information that follows or information you supply. Please print.

Call number: 82IL
Author: Edward Lear
Title: A Book of Nonsense
Publisher/Year: Museum of Art and Viking Press, 1980
Paulina Espada
54 Thorme Street
Bridgeport 06604
Madison School

BURROUGHS LIBRARY	Call number:
Author: _____	
Title: _____	
Publisher/Year: _____	
Correct and legible name and address required.	
Name _____	
Address _____	
City _____ ZIP _____	
School or Business _____	

EVALUATE Ask a friend to read and evaluate your writing.
Is the completed form legible?   Yes   No

DID YOU KNOW   English author and illustrator Edward Lear is known for his limericks.

EVALUATE

Pair students and have them discuss the legibility of their completed forms. Encourage them to make suggestions for improving legibility. (visual, auditory)

BEFORE WRITING

Discuss the function of a library call slip. Ask students to describe their last visit to a library and their method for finding a particular book they wanted.

MANUSCRIPT MAINTENANCE

Review the keys to legibility for manuscript writing: size and shape, slant, and spacing. Encourage students to follow these suggestions:

• Position the paper correctly.

• Pull the downstrokes in the proper direction.

• Shift the paper as your writing fills the space.

Right-handed students should pull downstrokes toward the midsection. Left-handed students should pull downstrokes toward the left elbow. Guide students in evaluating vertical quality. (visual, auditory, kinesthetic)

The form on page 33 is reproduced on Practice Master 12.

WRITE AWAY

Ask students to work together to compile an anthology of limericks, with each student contributing his or her favorite. Suggest students write the limerick they choose in manuscript or calligraphy.

COACHING HINT

Write the same word on the chalkboard in cursive and in manuscript. Use parallel lines of colored chalk to highlight the difference between manuscript verticality and cursive slant. (visual)

BEFORE WRITING

Ask students today's date. Invite them to respond in any language they know. Discuss the advantages of knowing more than one language. Invite a Spanish-speaking student to read aloud the Spanish words and expressions on the page.

WRITE AWAY

Point out that each date listed on page 34 may be a holiday. Labor Day sometimes falls on September 5, Thanksgiving on November 23, and Memorial Day on May 30. Martin Luther King, Jr.'s birthday is on January 15, June 14 is Flag Day, and April 1 is April Fool's Day. Invite students to write a short description of how they would like to spend one of the days. Students who speak Spanish might write in Spanish.

COACHING HINT

Writing rate will increase as students begin to move the writing hand more freely. To overcome finger motion, have students practice writing letters and words in a large size with crayon on folded newsprint. (kinesthetic)

Practice Masters 27–45 provide additional practice in writing in Spanish.

Write in Spanish

What is today's date?
¿Qué día es hoy?

Sunday January 19___	Wednesday February 19___
1	28

Monday	lunes
Tuesday	martes
Wednesday	miércoles
Thursday	jueves
Friday	viernes
Saturday	sábado
Sunday	domingo
January	enero
February	febrero
March	marzo
April	abril
May	mayo
June	junio
July	julio
August	agosto
September	septiembre
October	octubre
November	noviembre
December	diciembre

domingo.
1 de enero

miércoles.
28 de febrero

Write each date in Spanish. Use the word keys to help you.

Monday, September 5
lunes, 5 de septiembre

Thursday, November 23
jueves, 23 de noviembre

Sunday, January 15
domingo, 15 de enero

Tuesday, May 30
martes, 30 de mayo

Wednesday, June 14
miércoles, 14 de junio

Saturday, April 1
sábado, 1 de abril

On Your Own ¿Qué día es hoy? Answer in Spanish.

EVALUATE Did you use lowercase cursive letters? Yes No
Did you remember to include the accent marks? Yes No

34

EVALUATE

Ask students if their writing is legible. Have them explain why or why not. (visual, auditory)

¿Qué día es hoy? (keh DEE ah ehs oh=ee)
    lunes (LOO nehs)
    martes (MAHR tehs)
    miércoles (MEE=EHR coh lehs)
    jueves (HWEH vehs)
    viernes (VEE=EHR nehs)
    sábado (SAH bah doh)
    domingo (doh MEEN goh)
enero (eh NEH roh)
febrero (feh BREH roh)
marzo (MAHR soh)
abril (ah BREEL)
may (MAH yoh)
junio (HOO nee=oh)
julio (HOO lee=oh)
agosto (ah GOHS toh)
septiembre (sehp TEE=EHM breh)
octubre (ohk TOO breh)
noviembre (noh VEE=EHM breh)
diciembre (dee CEE=EHM breh)

Evaluate Size and Shape

A Fly and a Flea in a Flue

A fly and a flea in a flue
Were imprisoned, so what could they do?
Said the fly, "Let us flee!"
"Let us fly!" said the flea.
And they flew through a flaw in the flue.

Write this American limerick in your best handwriting.
Pay special attention to the size and shape of your letters.

_____

_____

_____

_____

_____

_____

_____

_____

_____

EVALUATE Are your tall letters all the same height?   Yes   No
Are your short letters half the height of your tall letters?   Yes   No
Did you avoid collisions?   Yes   No

35

EVALUATE

Guide students through the self-evaluation process, focusing on size and shape. Ask them to describe ways they might improve their writing. If necessary, have them rewrite the limerick, aiming for their personal best. (visual, auditory)

Certificates of Progress should be awarded to those students who show notable handwriting progress and Certificates of Excellence to those who progress to the top levels of handwriting proficiency.

KEYS TO LEGIBILITY: SIZE AND SHAPE

Review the cursive alphabet with students, helping them group the letters according to size.

- Tall letters should not touch the headline. Lowercase b, d, f, h, k, l, and t are tall. All uppercase letters are tall.

- Short letters are half the height of tall letters. Lowercase a, c, e, g, i, j, m, n, o, p, q, r, s, u, v, w, x, y, and z are short.

- Letters with descenders extend below the baseline. Lowercase f, g, j, p, q, y, and z have descenders. Uppercase J, Y, and Z have descenders.

Provide opportunities to practice proper placement of each letter on handwriting guidelines. (visual, auditory, kinesthetic)

WRITE AWAY

Point out that the rhyming pattern for "A Fly and a Flea in a Flue" is AABBA (lines 1, 2, and 5 rhyme; lines 3 and 4 rhyme). Invite students to work in small groups to write their own limericks with the same rhyming pattern.

COACHING HINT

Right-handed teachers will better understand the stroke, visual perspective, and posture of left-handed students if they practice the left-handed position themselves.

Keys to Legibility: Uniform Slant

Follow these suggestions to write with uniform slant.

**POSITION
PULL
SHIFT**

Check your paper position.
Pull your downstrokes in the proper direction.
Shift your paper as you write.

If you are left-handed . . .

pull toward your left elbow.

If you are right-handed . . .

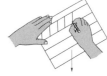

pull toward your midsection.

Write these words and the places they are named for. Try to make your slant uniform.

cashmere (Kashmir, India)

cologne (Cologne, Germany)

denim (Nîmes, France)

hamburger (Hamburg, Germany)

EVALUATE Check your slant.

Draw lines through the slant strokes of the letters.

Your slant should look like ⟍⟍⟍, not ⟍⟋⟍.

36

MODEL THE WRITING

Remind students that, in cursive writing, letters slant to the right. Show an example of correct slant by writing *uniform* on guidelines. Invite a volunteer to check the slant of your writing by drawing lines through the slant strokes of the letters. These lines should slant forward and be parallel. (visual, auditory, kinesthetic)

EVALUATE

Guide students through the self-evaluation process. Then ask if the words they wrote are easy to read. Encourage them to explain why or why not. (visual, auditory)

Keys to Legibility: Correct Spacing

These letters, words, and sentences are legible. The spacing is correct.

Between Letters There should be space for *O*.
Between Words There should be space for \ .
Between Sentences There should be space for *O*.

a stone building O King Mausolus

Write about the origin of the word *mausoleum*. For correct spacing, shift your paper as you write.

A mausoleum is a large tomb, usually a stone building. The first mausoleum was built around 353 BC for King Mausolus, ruler of Caria. It is one of the Seven Wonders of the Ancient World.

EVALUATE Is there space for *O* between letters?   Yes   No

Is there space for \ between words?   Yes   No

Is there space for *O* between sentences?   Yes   No

37

MODEL THE WRITING

To show an example of correct spacing, write the following sentences on guidelines: *The ancient Greeks listed memorable things travelers should see. The ancient Romans did, too.* Invite volunteers to check the spacing by drawing ovals between letters, by drawing slanted lines between words, and by writing uppercase **O** between sentences. (visual, auditory, kinesthetic)

EVALUATE

Guide students through the self-evaluation process. Then ask if their paragraph is easy to read. Encourage them to explain why or why not. (visual, auditory)

BEFORE WRITING

On the chalkboard, write these two simple sentences: *Many people are vegetarians. Most people eat meat.* Demonstrate how to use a comma and the word *but* to combine the sentences.

KEYS TO LEGIBILITY: UNIFORM SLANT

Review the hints for writing with uniform slant (POSITION, PULL, SHIFT). Help students position their papers correctly and check the direction of their strokes. (visual, auditory, kinesthetic)

WRITE AWAY

Would students like to taste bird's nest soup, or would they like to eat a thousand-year-old egg? Ask students to write a paragraph describing their choice and reasons supporting their choice.

Practice Masters 46–53 provide practice in writing across the curriculum.

Write Compound Sentences

Two simple sentences can be combined to form a compound sentence.

In China, bird's nest soup is a delicacy, and a thousand-year-old egg is a tasty appetizer.

Use a comma and the word in parentheses to combine each pair of sentences.

The soup is actually made from a bird's nest. The egg is not really a thousand years old. (but)

Would you like to try bird's nest soup? Would you prefer a thousand-year-old egg? (or)

On Your Own Write a compound sentence.

EVALUATE Does your writing have uniform slant? Yes No

EVALUATE

After students have evaluated their slant, ask if their writing is legible. Have them explain why or why not. (visual, auditory)

Write Complex Sentences

Two sentences can be combined to form a complex sentence.

Do as the Romans do when you're in Rome.

Use the word in parentheses to combine each pair of sentences.

It is not considered rude to stare at other people.
You are in Pakistan. (if)

_____

_____

_____

Polite Japanese women cover their mouths.
They laugh. (when)

_____

_____

A horizontal shake of the head means "no."
You are in Sri Lanka or Bulgaria. (unless)

_____

_____

_____

On Your Own Write a complex sentence. Use the connecting word *because*.

_____

_____

EVALUATE Is there space for *o* between letters?   Yes   No
Is there space for \ between words?   Yes   No

39

BEFORE WRITING

On the chalkboard, write these two simple sentences: *You can snap your fingers to applaud. You are in Spain.* Demonstrate how to use the word *if* to combine the sentences.

KEYS TO LEGIBILITY: CORRECT SPACING

Remind students that shifting their papers as they write can help keep spacing consistent. (visual, kinesthetic)

WRITE AWAY

Ask students to write about body language in the United States. Suggest they explain the meaning of such gestures as a shrug of the shoulders, a nod of the head, and a hug.

EVALUATE

After students have evaluated the spacing between their letters and their words, ask if their writing is legible. Have them explain why or why not. (visual, auditory)

BEFORE WRITING

Share the following information with students: Auguste Rodin is considered by many to be the greatest sculptor of the 1800s. Like Michelangelo, he created human figures noted for their great emotional intensity.

KEYS TO LEGIBILITY: UNIFORM SLANT

Evaluate slant by drawing lines through the slant strokes of the letters. The lines should be parallel and should show uniform forward slant. (visual, kinesthetic)

Write About a Sculpture

This statue, called "The Thinker," is one of French sculptor Auguste Rodin's most famous works. Think like the Thinker and list some ideas he may be thinking about. Write your ideas beneath the headings *People, Places, Things,* and *Ideas.*

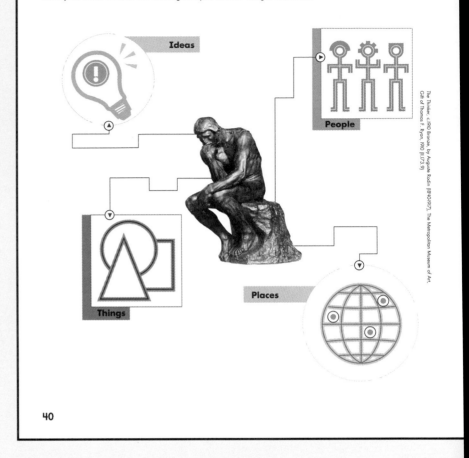

Ideas

People

Things

Places

The Thinker, c.1910, Bronze, by Auguste Rodin (1840-1917), The Metropolitan Museum of Art, Gift of Thomas F. Ryan, 1910 (11.173.9)

40

EVALUATE

Ask students to evaluate the legibility of their notes, reminding them that the notes are for their own use. Suggest they cross out and rewrite any words they might find hard to read later. (visual, auditory, kinesthetic)

What is going on in the Thinker's mind? Share your ideas about what he may be thinking. Write in the first person, using the pronoun *I*.

**LEGIBLE
LETTERS**   Shift your paper as you write.

_____

_____

_____

_____

_____

_____

_____

_____

_____

_____

_____

_____

_____

_____

_____

_____

_____

EVALUATE Is the slant uniform?   Yes   No
           Is your spacing correct?   Yes   No

41

EVALUATE

After students have evaluated their writing, have them describe what they did to make their slant uniform and their spacing correct. Encourage them to make suggestions for improving legibility. (visual, auditory)

WRITE AWAY

Invite students to enter into a dialogue with "The Thinker." Have them record their conversations. Participate by suggesting an opening line, such as "'Excuse me, sir,' I said, tapping the man on his shoulder."

COACHING HINT

As students near the end of their handwriting texts, it is important to recognize and acknowledge the improvement they have made. Comparing students' writing with samples from the beginning of the year provides motivation for further progress, particularly for students who have had difficulties with handwriting.

BEFORE WRITING

Review calendar terms in Spanish on page 34. Unlike English, Spanish and French do not capitalize the names of days and months. In Spanish, the word *of* is used between the date and the month. In French, *the* is used before the date. Invite a French-speaking student to read aloud the French words and expressions on the page.

KEYS TO LEGIBILITY: CORRECT SPACING

Remind students there should be enough space for $\mathcal{O}$ between letters, \ between words, and $\mathcal{O}$ between sentences. (visual, auditory)

WRITE AWAY

Ask students to write a paragraph telling which language besides English they would like to know well and why. Students who speak a second language might write in that language.

Write in French

What is today's date?
Quelle est la date aujourd'hui?

Sunday	Wednesday
January 19___	February 19___
I	**28**

		dimanche.	mercredi.
		le 1 janvier	le 28 février

Monday	lundi
Tuesday	mardi
Wednesday	mercredi
Thursday	jeudi
Friday	vendredi
Saturday	samedi
Sunday	dimanche

January	janvier
February	février
March	mars
April	avril
May	mai
June	juin
July	juillet
August	août
September	septembre
October	octobre
November	novembre
December	décembre

Write each date in French. Use the word keys to help you.

Monday, September 5
lundi, le 5 septembre

Thursday, November 23
jeudi, le 23 novembre

Sunday, January 15
dimanche, le 15 janvier

Tuesday, May 30
mardi, le 30 mai

Wednesday, June 14
mercredi, le 14 juin

Saturday, April 1
samedi, le 1 avril

On Your Own Quelle est la date aujourd'hui? Answer in French.

_____

EVALUATE Is the slant uniform? Yes No
Is your spacing correct? Yes No

42

EVALUATE

After students have evaluated their slant and spacing, ask if their writing is legible. Have them explain why or why not. (visual, auditory)

Quelle est la date aujourd'hui? (kehl eh lah daht oh zhoor DWEE)
  Lundi (luhn DEE)
  mardi (mar DEE)
  mercredi (mer kruh DEE)
  jeudi (zhoo DEE)
  vendredi (vahn druh DEE)
  samedi (sahm DEE)
  dimanche (dee MAHNSH)
  janvier (zhahn VYAY)
  février (fay VRYAY)
  mars (MARS)
  avril (ah VREEL)
  mai (MEH)
  juin (ZHWAN)
  juillet (zhwee YEH)
  août (OO)
  septembre (sep TAHN br)
  octobre (awk TAW br)
  novembre (naw VAHN br)
  decembre (day SAHN br)

Manuscript Maintenance

Label the seven continents on the map below. Write in manuscript. Use these facts to help you.

The Seven Continents

- **Asia**, the world's largest continent, is in the Eastern Hemisphere.
- **Europe**, the second smallest continent, is actually a peninsula that extends westward from northwestern Asia.
- **Africa**, the second largest continent, is south of Europe.
- **North America**, the continent with the longest coastline, is in the Western Hemisphere.
- **Antarctica**, the coldest and emptiest continent, is located near the South Pole.
- **Australia**, the smallest continent, is an island in the Southern Hemisphere.
- **South America**, the fourth largest continent, is located near the South Pole.

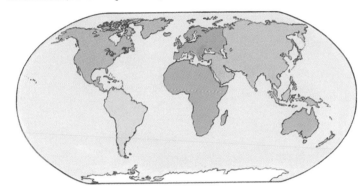

EVALUATE Are your labels legible?   Yes   No

  DID YOU KNOW?   Australia is the only continent made up of a single country.

43

EVALUATE

Have students focus on spacing to determine whether their manuscript letters are legible. Discuss ways to improve legibility. (visual, auditory)

BEFORE WRITING

On a map of the world, locate the prime meridian and ask students to identify the Eastern and Western Hemispheres. Locate the equator and ask students to identify the Northern and Southern Hemispheres.

MANUSCRIPT MAINTENANCE

Review the keys to legibility for manuscript writing: size and shape, slant, and spacing. Show an example of correct spacing between letters, words, and sentences. Remind students that letters and words too close together or too far apart make writing difficult to read. Provide opportunities for students to practice good spacing. (visual, auditory, kinesthetic)

WRITE AWAY

Ask students to compile a list of interesting facts about the seven continents. For example, Europe has no desert, and Antarctica has no country. Students can use an almanac or an encyclopedia as a source of information.

COACHING HINT

To reinforce manuscript writing, have students use manuscript to prepare invitations to parties, to send holiday greetings, and to label maps and diagrams.

BEFORE WRITING

Discuss handwriting in colonial America. Point out that penmanship was considered one of the most important subjects in school. Students would generally spend an entire morning copying a word or phrase written by the teacher at the top of their slates or papers. Students also kept copybooks in which they wrote a proverb of the day.

WRITE AWAY

Have students keep a copybook for the week. Suggest that each day they write a proverb, saying, or rule in their book. To get students started, share several additional rules from George Washington's list: Rule 3: "Show nothing to your friend that might affright him." Rule 4: "In the presence of others sing not to yourself with humming noise, nor drum with your fingers or feet."

COACHING HINT

Use the keys to legibility as hints for frequent handwriting evaluation in all curriculum areas. Display students' handwriting examples that show excellence. (visual)

Personal Style

Study the handwriting of George Washington (1732–1799) and young poet Phillis Wheatley (1753–1784).

6.th Sleep not when others Speak, Si b not when others stand, Speak not when you should hold your Peace, walk not on when others Stop — George Washington, age 12

While an intrinsic ardor bids me write The muse doth promise to assist my pen. — Phillis Wheatley, age 13

How is their handwriting alike? Do you see any differences?

_____

_____

_____

LEGIBLE LETTERS

Personal differences are acceptable as long as your handwriting is legible.

Choose one of the selections and write it in your own personal style.

_____

_____

_____

_____

EVALUATE Ask a friend to read your writing.
Is it legible? Yes No

DID YOU KNOW Born in Africa and brought to America as a slave, Phillis Wheatley learned to speak, read, and write English in less than two years.

44

EVALUATE

Pair students and have them discuss their personal styles. Encourage them to experiment with different handwriting styles, reminding them to keep their writing legible. (visual, auditory, kinesthetic)

Evaluate Slant and Spacing

Weather

Whether the weather be fine
Or whether the weather be not.
Whether the weather be cold
Or whether the weather be hot.
We'll weather the weather
Whatever the weather.
Whether we like it or not.

Write this British tongue twister in your best handwriting.
Pay special attention to slant and spacing.

EVALUATE Does your writing have uniform slant?	Yes	No
Is there space for $\mathcal{O}$ between letters?	Yes	No
Is there space for $\diagdown$ between words?	Yes	No

45

EVALUATE

Guide students through the self-evaluation process, focusing on slant and spacing. Ask whether improvement is needed. If necessary, have them rewrite the tongue twister, aiming for their personal best. (visual, auditory)

Certificates of Progress *should be awarded to those students who show notable handwriting progress and* Certificates of Excellence *to those who progress to the top levels of handwriting proficiency.*

KEYS TO LEGIBILITY: UNIFORM SLANT

Remind students that in cursive writing all letters should slant to the right. Review the hints for writing with uniform slant for both left-handed and right-handed writers.

- **Position your paper correctly.**
- **Pull the downstrokes in the proper direction.**
- **Shift your paper to the left as you write.**

Invite both left-handed and right-handed students to model for classmates. (visual, auditory, kinesthetic)

KEYS TO LEGIBILITY: CORRECT SPACING

Display examples of correct spacing between letters, words, and sentences.

Between Letters There should be enough space for $\mathcal{O}$.
Between Words There should be enough space for $\diagdown$.
Between Sentences There should be enough space for $\bigcirc$.

Provide opportunities for students to write two or more sentences and to check the spacing between letters, words, and sentences. (auditory, visual, kinesthetic)

WRITE AWAY

Invite students to compile an anthology of tongue twisters, with each student contributing one page. Suggest students write either their favorite tongue twister or a tongue twister of their own.

POSTTEST

Remind students that on page 5 as a pretest they wrote the first stanza of this poem and evaluated their handwriting. They will write the same stanza for the posttest. Tell them to use correct letter size and shape, uniform slant, and correct spacing as they write. (visual, auditory, kinesthetic)

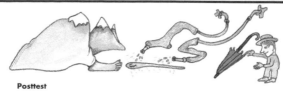

Posttest
Have You Ever Seen?

Have you ever seen a sheet on a river bed?
Or a single hair from a hammer's head?
Has the foot of a mountain any toes?
And is there a pair of garden hose?

Does the needle ever wink its eye?
Why doesn't the wing of a building fly?
Can you tickle the ribs of a parasol?
Or open the trunk of a tree at all?

Are the teeth of a rake ever going to bite?
Have the hands of a clock any left or right?
Can the garden plot be deep and dark?
And what is the sound of the birch's bark?

On your paper, write the first stanza of this poem in your best cursive handwriting.

EVALUATE Is your writing legible?   Yes   No

46

EVALUATE

Have students use the keys to legibility to evaluate their handwriting. Suggest they compare this writing with their writing on the pretest. Discuss how their writing has changed. Meet individually with students to help them assess their progress. (visual, auditory)

Record of Student's Handwriting Skills

Cursive

	Needs Improvement	Shows Mastery
Sits correctly	☐	☐
Holds pencil correctly	☐	☐
Positions paper correctly	☐	☐
Writes undercurve letters: **i, t, u, w**	☐	☐
Writes undercurve letters: **r, s, p, j**	☐	☐
Writes downcurve letters: **a, c, d, q, g, o**	☐	☐
Writes overcurve letters: **n, m, x, y, z, v**	☐	☐
Writes letters with loops: **e, l, h, k, f, b**	☐	☐
Writes downcurve letters: **A, C, E, O**	☐	☐
Writes curve forward letters: **N, M, K, H**	☐	☐
Writes curve forward letters: **U, Y, Z, V, X, W**	☐	☐
Writes doublecurve letters: **T, F**	☐	☐
Writes overcurve letters: **I, Q, J**	☐	☐
Writes letters with loops: **G, S, L, D**	☐	☐
Writes undercurve-slant letters: **P, B, R**	☐	☐
Writes numerals **1–10**	☐	☐
Writes the undercurve to undercurve joining	☐	☐
Writes the undercurve to downcurve joining	☐	☐
Writes the undercurve to overcurve joining	☐	☐
Writes the overcurve to undercurve joining	☐	☐
Writes the overcurve to downcurve joining	☐	☐
Writes the overcurve to overcurve joining	☐	☐
Writes the checkstroke to undercurve joining	☐	☐
Writes the checkstroke to downcurve joining	☐	☐
Writes the checkstroke to overcurve joining	☐	☐
Writes with correct size and shape	☐	☐
Writes with uniform slant	☐	☐
Writes with correct spacing	☐	☐
Writes quickly	☐	☐
Shows development in personal style	☐	☐

47

The form on page 47 is reproduced on Practice Master 13.

COACHING HINT
If a student needs improvement, reevaluate his or her writing following practice over a period of time. Invite the student to share in the evaluation. (visual, auditory)

EVALUATE

This chart provides a place for you to record the student's handwriting progress. The chart lists the essential skills in the program. After each skill has been practiced and evaluated, you can indicate whether the student *Shows Mastery* or *Needs Improvement* by checking the appropriate box.

Shows Mastery Mastery of written letterforms is achieved when the student writes the letters using correct basic strokes. Compare the student's written letterforms with the letter models. Keep in mind the keys to legibility (size and shape, slant, and spacing) when evaluating letters, numerals, punctuation marks, words, and sentences.

Needs Improvement If a student has not mastered a skill, provide additional basic instruction and practice. To improve letterforms, have the student practice writing the letter in isolation and within words and sentences. Reinforce instruction through activities geared to the student's modality strengths. When mastery of the skill is achieved, check *Shows Mastery*.

Index